STUDY GUIDE

A Biblical Concepts Bible
Study Based on the Novel

OVER MY DEAD BODY

KELLY FITZGERALD FOWLER

A Biblical Concepts Study Guide Based on the Novel Over My Dead Body, by Kelly Fitzgerald Fowler.

RPP

Relevant
Pages Press

Published by Relevant Pages Press, Charleston, South Carolina.

Cover design by: Moondog Animation Studio, Cyril Jedor and Suzanne Parada

Study Guide Design by: MacKenzie Fowler and James Milton

Interior Layout by: Judge Fowler

Editor: Janet Schwind

Printed in the United States of America.

A Note from the Author

Dear friends,

It brings me great joy to know you have chosen to dig deeper into the biblical concepts in the novel *Over My Dead Body*. I pray my passion for these topics and the word of God will come across in my written word. This study guide is for the person who has read the novel and wants to learn more about the significant biblical concepts in the story. One central theme is the supernatural aspects of the Father, Son, and Holy Spirit. Come along with me as I walk you through some interesting topics you may not typically hear about at church but you will discover as you dig deeper.

I look forward to exploring them together.

A bit about me: I am a child of God who grew up the youngest of four girls in a, classic Irish-American Catholic family. Proud mother of two daughters and Gigi to a grandson and a granddaughter. I was born in Omaha, Nebraska, but have lived in the Charleston, South Carolina, area since 1997. You will learn more about my journey as we move through the study guide, but know I'm praying for you to grow your faith by leaps and bounds as you set aside time to learn more about these supernatural topics.

Love and blessings,

Kelly Fitzgerald Fowler

❖ If you are leading a group through this study please see the last page for ideas, insights and directions from me.

For My Family,
with Love.
Dig Deep!

Table of Contents

Chapter 1

WRITING WITH GOD

I started on my journey to write *Over My Dead Body: A Supernatural Novel* in 2007. I was attending a conference in Atlanta where the speaker and senior associate leader at Bethel Church Kris Vallotton said that Jesus had said, "Over my dead body will you go to hell" and "You have a choice if you will go to hell or not. Jesus chose heaven for you."

The idiom "over my dead body" stuck with me for a long time, and I started thinking about a conversation in heaven between the Father, Jesus and the Holy Spirit on this very topic. I recorded in Chapter Two what I imagined that conversation may have been like if you would like to review. Chapter Two of this study guide will dig into this topic as well.

In the meantime, my thoughts and personal Bible study moved to the High Priest Annas (also Ananus or Ananias first mentioned in Luke 3:2). We will study him in-depth later, but I imagined Annas was most likely there to witness the crucifixion when Jesus said out loud, "Forgive them for they know not what they do." The thought and understanding that Jesus only did what he saw the Father doing (John 5:10-20) made me think Annas, the overseer of the first of six illegal trials, could very well be in heaven. Jesus asked for forgiveness for all those present. With those Scriptures in mind, I concluded the Father directed Jesus to pray for forgiveness for all present.

I kept hearing the phrase "Over my dead body" running through my head from the Holy Spirit. After several months of hearing it as well as seeing 11:11 twice a day, I asked, "What do you want me to do, Lord?"

His answer was clear: "It's a book. Write it!"

What? It took me a while to accept the challenge. Writing a book was on my bucket list from when I was 22, but I didn't mean it. Let's face it—it is a ton of work (be careful what you ask for). I hesitated for a long time but concluded the Holy Spirit was going to keep bringing the idea to the surface.

As soon as I got serious about writing, tons of obstacles stood in my way (I will write about this spiritual warfare later also). You know the saying "the hounds of hell stand at the door to your destiny," another Kris Vallotton classic quote. Anyway, the prodding by the Holy Spirit was relentless. So I sat down and pounded the keyboard for the last ten years to finally finish the story in 2018. These last two years of the ten were laser-focused since my youngest went off to college.

Through the writing process my heart exploded with a greater realization of the love of Jesus. The book title comes from what I imagine are the intentions of his heart when he offered up his body as a living sacrifice for us. He may not literally have said, "Over my dead body will you go to hell," but what he did for us said it loud and clear.

This book is for everyone because Jesus died for humanity, but I hope it will especially reach these four specific groups of people:

1. For the Christian who has not discovered that Jesus called you to take the gospel to Jerusalem first. Read Romans 11:11 and Acts 1:8. Jesus gave clear direction to witness to Jerusalem, Judea, and Samaria **and then** to the ends of the earth. The path is clear to start in Jerusalem, not because he wants you to be and act Jewish, but because his plan included his chosen people.

2. For the Jewish person who has never explored or dug into the Jewish books of the New Testament. Israelites

wrote the books of both the Old and New Testament. They are for the Jewish people to explore.

3. For the person who has experienced the Holy Spirit in dreams and visions. Much of the experiences of my main characters have been from my own experiences. I see the throne room with flowing purple robes to the sky in a vision and in my quiet time often. The Holy Spirit directs me through dreams and God's word just like all of those in the Bible who heard from the Lord in dreams—Mary, Joseph, David, Solomon, and Job, to name a few. So, be encouraged that you can listen to the voice of the Lord in this way, too, but confirm everything in his Scriptures.

4. For the person who thinks they are a lost cause. Read the book. Jesus is the God of second, third, and fourth chances. Be encouraged; it is never too late to turn around. You can change your mind. He will take you back no matter what deals you made with yourself or what lies you were tricked into believing from the enemy of your soul.

My goal of this Bible study is to help answer any biblical concept questions readers might have from reading the novel.

In each chapter, I will be sharing the personal supernatural experiences I have had with the Holy Spirit. I share them to inspire you to want the abundant life Jesus promised and to provoke you to dream more with God. The word of God says he is no respecter of persons (Romans 2:11), which means if he does it for me, he will do it for you. I know your next question is how? How can I walk in this supernatural lifestyle? My answer to you will always be by studying God's word. I pray your time in this study will lead you into a higher understanding of your authority and the abundance Jesus planned for you before the very foundations of the earth. Once you understand your authority and walk in it, you will have a new awakening about walking in the supernatural.

In the summertime as a kid, my mother would send us to vacation Bible school (VBS) at the Baptist church. She had grown up Baptist and converted to Catholicism when she married my dad. I was exposed to the gospel as a child and accepted Jesus at age seven, but there was little opportunity to be discipled once VBS ended.

My grandmother was a spirit-filled Catholic. I didn't realize she was spirit-filled until she was already in heaven, but she walked in the power of the Holy Spirit from her involvement with Koinonia, which is a group of Christians from several denominations who celebrated what they could all agree on about Christ. That same summer I met Jesus. I told my grandmother I suffered from horrendous nightmares. She asked if I prayed the Lord's Prayer before I went to sleep. My answer was no, but from that day forward, I prayed it every day I remembered, and the nightmares left me. So, you can see the enemy was inflicting fear on me as a young child, and prayer broke it off, which taught me prayer keeps the enemy away. However, we lived 600 miles away from my grandmother, so her influence was in little doses. My parents stuck to a more traditional Catholic approach, which meant you go to church, do good, and hope when you get to check out of this life, you have enough good works to get you into heaven. Getting into heaven for them was more about earning your way in, and I had no idea what "accepting Jesus" actually meant.

At VBS, I got to be with other kids and learn about Jesus— the fun Jesus. Back then, my church didn't have children's programs. We were disciplined to sit still for an hour every Sunday on a hard pew (I know...poor Kelly). The worst part was I had to listen to stories and concepts way over my head and was expected to pay attention. My parents knew it was boring. How do I know this, you ask? As soon as my oldest sister could drive, my parents started sending us to church without them. I learned going to church was something you did when you had little kids. It was tradition, a religion, not a relationship with the living God. As a pre-teen, I decided I would not attend church as an adult. I had a discussion with my grandmother about this, and to this day I am sure she prayed for me on overdrive, which would explain why my church life is so fulfilling today. Thank God for a praying grandmother.

My second experience with the supernatural was when the enemy went after my parents' marriage. Once my family fell apart, the enemy whispered in my ear, "They don't care about you!" There is a ripple effect of the enemy going after marriages. I ran away from home twice; each time it was clear how the evil preyed upon my age and naivety with several dangerous situations. The enemy had a plan to ruin my life and me.

God had different plans for us all. I like to take Scripture and dig into the meaning of words and put them in my own words. You can look this Scripture up in whatever version you prefer; here is what I found from digging deeper into the meaning of Jeremiah 29: 11-14, in my own words:

I know what I, the Lord, have stored up for you, Kelly (Put your name in there too)! I have plans to prosper you, Kelly, for my purposes. I would never let any harm come to you, (Kelly...you get the idea). I have supernatural plans for you to have a future you could never have imagined on your own. Then, say my name (I AM, Father, Papa, Holy Spirit, Jesus... choose one of my many names) when you want to have a conversation with me. I will hear every word spoken and unspoken. There is not one thought of yours I will not know. When you take your entire mind, will, emotions and even that tiny brain I put in your heart to find me (did you know scientist have proven there is a flesh part of the heart that acts similar to a brain inside your heart? See *Switch on your Brain* by Dr. Carolyn Leaf), I promise you will find me. I, the Lord declare, "The enemy will not rake you over the coals ever again!"

Although this was a message given to Jeremiah for Israel, I use this to remind myself that I can be led into captivity just like they were. God led them into captivity due to their disobedience. I am onto the schemes of the enemy and use Scripture and the name of the Lord Jesus Christ as a sword to defeat the liar so I can be set free.

If God has a plan for you (which he does), I guarantee the enemy has a plan for you. If the Lord is not your shepherd, then someone else is shepherding you.

As a young adult, I married at 19 and was divorced by 21. The same lying spirit who went after my parents attacked me. I also failed the test, but God gave both me and my parents a chance to turn around. I have now been married for 23 years to the love of my life and my parents just got remarried after being divorced for 35 years! Back then I found myself a single parent and needed Jesus more than ever. I attended a meeting where there was supernatural activity and got fully baptized in the Holy Spirit. I had never experienced anything like it before. I knew nothing about being baptized by the Holy Spirit (Acts 1:4-5). Imagine my surprise when I received the evidence of the baptism with a spiritual language referred to as the gift of speaking in tongues (1 Corinthians 12:7). It broke out like it did on the day of Pentecost in the book of Acts. I recently learned through the counsel of the Holy Spirit, the nine spiritual gifts and nine fruits of the Spirit are available to every believer. If you have the spiritual gift of faith, then you should easily believe you can receive any of the other gifts of the Spirit. The Spirit of Jesus can give you any of the gifts any time he wants. There is nothing wrong with asking him for them either, although most gifts are given out of love and many people, including myself, are thrilled with the gift of faith. Jesus said in Matthew 7:7, ask, knock (keep asking) and you shall receive. If you want the gift of operating in signs and wonders, ask! If you want to be able to discern spirits like Naomi in the novel, ask! Then believe you could receive it as easily as you believed Jesus was who he said he was when the Holy Spirit gave you the incredible supernatural gift of faith. Paul even says for those who have the gift of tongues to ask for the gift of interpretation of tongues in 1 Corinthians 14:13. Anyway, this was a whole new level of spiritual activity for me and started me on a seeking journey, which is still going strong today. After years and years of supernatural activity surrounding my life, I am still learning and sharing, with the hope that others will draw closer to God on their journey.

Keep your mind fixed on the mind of Christ on your journey through the biblical concepts from the novel. These concepts reveal my walk with plenty of Scripture for backup. I pray you too will be able to walk into the supernatural with no hesitation once you read what God's word says about these concepts. I hope this study will make some difficult and rarely discussed ideas from the Bible come alive for you. I pray the Holy Spirit will touch you and reach you so you can reach others with his truth.

Let's dig in!

Discussion Questions

1. Do you know Jesus or just know about Jesus? What do you think is the difference? Read Isaiah 52:13, Isaiah 53:12 and Psalm: 22. (Old Testament). Romans: 5: 8, Romans. 6:23, John 3:16 and 1 John 4:10 (New Testament).

2. Have you been baptized in the Holy Spirit? If not, what questions do you have about the topic? Read 1 Samuel 10:5-7, Psalm 51:11, Saul and David. Throughout the Old Testament, the Spirit rests upon people. New Testament, before Jesus resurrected. Read Luke 1:35, Matthew 3:14. The book of John is all about Jesus being baptized in the Spirit even though he already had the Spirit in his mother's womb. Read Acts 1:1-1:8. The entire book is about being baptized to do the work of the Holy Spirit.

3. Have you ever had a supernatural experience? If so, share the details with the group.

Chapter 2

THRONE ROOM OF HEAVEN

When I think about the supernatural, one of the first things I think about is the throne room in heaven. I want to briefly share a bit about my experience of what I would consider a throne room visit. Years ago, I participated in soaking prayer at a local church. The first time I was there resting in the presence of God, I started to experience a purple flowing sensation. I didn't know what the sensation was or what was causing it. It was a brand new experience for me, but I wanted to know because it was supernatural. Soaking prayer lasted from nine until noon on Fridays. The time spent there felt like ten minutes. It was unlike anything I've ever experienced before in my life. Experiencing supernatural time in his courts is an experience I hope everyone will consider trying at home and ten minutes before reading each chapter of this study if you are not being led in a classroom while going through this study. Turn on some soaking music (search online for this type of music). I recommend Cathy Mart Music or Grace Williams.

Anyway, I started pressing into the Lord in prayer and asked him what this purple flowing substance of light was and why does it seem like I'm only there for ten minutes but yet it's a three-hour prayer time? The Lord answered and said, "Kelly, the purple substance is my robe and the reason you feel like you're only there for ten minutes is because one day in my courts is like a thousand elsewhere (2 Peter 3:8). This started me on a journey of wanting to know more about the throne room, and it's the reason why I included it in my novel. The throne room of heaven as described by Daniel 7:9-10:

> "As I looked, thrones were set in place, and the Ancient of Days took his seat. His clothing was as white as snow; the hair of his head was white like wool. His throne was flaming with fire, and its wheels were all ablaze. A river of fire was flowing coming out from before him. Thousands upon thousands attended him; ten thousand times ten thousand stood before him. The court was seated, and the books opened."

If you have read Chapter Two in *Over My Dead Body*, this scene should sound familiar to you already. What I imagined took place there between the Trinity is very much part of my novel. You can talk more about books in heaven in your discussion time today as I have added a discussion question regarding the books in heaven's library. I pray all your names be written in the Book of Life and you and your discussion today will be recorded in the book of remembrance, or fondly referred to as God's coffee table book.

Discussion Questions

1. What does the Bible say about the throne room of heaven? Read Daniel 7:9-10, Revelation 4 (whole chapter).

2. Have you ever had any supernatural experience in any of the rooms in heaven? In John 14:2, Jesus said, "In my Father's house there are many rooms." Have you pondered other rooms in heaven?

3. Have you considered the library in heaven? There is the Book of Life and the Book of Remembrance (God's coffee table book is what I call it, Malachi 3:16), so there must be a room in heaven that holds the books called a library. Read Revelation 3:5 and Philippians 4:3 3 (the Book of Life), Daniel 10:20-21 (the Book of Truth). Discuss what you think the library in heaven is like.

4. Have you ever had an experience where time flies at the speed of sound like I mentioned in my above account of the throne room? Describe. Read Psalm 84:10, 2 Peter 3:8 -9, Ephesians 5:15-17.

What does this mean for you?

You can experience the throne room of heaven too. If he did it for me, Daniel and Paul, he will do it for you also! After you study these passages, you can ask the Lord to help you experience this for yourself. Tell him you want to experience his throne room. Make-believe (meaning make yourself believe) you are in the throne room by using your God-given imagination. I am beginning to believe dreaming and thinking about heaven is one of the real reasons God gave us imagination. So you can go wherever you want to go in your mind. Writing this book was a way of me being able to play out an outcome, which started in my imagination. Yes, it's a novel, but without imagination, the creative process is cut off, and destiny is untouchable.

Here is how I started. I picture myself as a child on Papa God's lap on the throne. I see myself running my fingers through the beard of the Father, which for some reason has oil dripping from it. I do this anytime I need to be comforted by my heavenly Father or, quite frankly, want to go on an adventure in heaven. He looks at me with love, and when I look at him all I can see is his beard and a bunch of light, but it comforts me to have this type of relationship with the Father. There is a treasure trove of visions from heaven you can use if you dig in Scripture for hints. While on his lap, look down at his feet and see him using the earth for a footstool. Get alone with God and write about what you see in your imagination and then ask him to confirm what he showed you in Scripture. The Lord is not afraid to confirm anything for you if you ask.

Chapter 3

ANGELS

I always thought it would be amazing to meet an angel in person. Then one day, I had this incredible dream. I was in a lovely old-fashioned little white country church worshiping the Lord when I looked up, and there was a humongous blue angel that stood three floors tall at the front of the church. I immediately fell to my knees in fear. I covered my face because it scared me so much. The next scene was my husband and I sitting on a bench just outside with the little white church in the distance. We were talking to each other.

I asked my husband, "Did you see the enormous blue angel?"

He said, "Yes, I saw it; I shook hands with it."

I looked over at him wide-eyed and said, "You are so brave!"

Less than one week after this dream encounter, my husband had a cardiac arrest. The heart problem, as we found out three years later, was brought on from a disease called sarcoidosis. We had been at a Christmas party and on our way home, he pulled the car over, got out and walked to the grass. It looked like he was going to throw up, but he just fell over onto the ground. I called 911 immediately while a friend of ours who saw him fall jumped out of his rolling truck and ran to give him CPR. I was in hysterics on the phone with the 911 operator. The Holy Spirit told me at that moment to pray these words: "He shall live and not die and declare the works of the Lord," a Scripture I did not know by heart (Psalm 118:17). The next thing I knew, I was sitting in ICU, watching him fight for his life. One of the nurses even said I should not bring my daughter in to see him with all those tubes in his body so it would not be the last thing she ever saw of her dad. When she said that, I canceled her words in the name of Jesus. Jesus told me before I got there that my husband would live, and I believed him. Don't ever let people speak death over your loved ones.

I had the peace of the Holy Spirit; you know the peace that surpasses all your understanding. I walked to my husband to kiss him on the forehead and looked at a sheet the hospital had put on him for warmth and saw the word Angelica in massive blue ink. My sweet Holy Spirit immediately flashed back to remind me of the dream about the enormous blue angel. Remember, in the dream I was fearful, but my husband had just shaken hands with the angel. He was so courageous. The flashback to the dream confirmed for me he would make it through. That was an angelic encounter from my dream the Lord brought to my mind to comfort me.

The blue angel dream is also the dream that keeps on giving. For my birthday a couple of years ago I chose a trip to Peggy Cove, Canada. As we drove toward one of the most beautiful lighthouses in history, there sat the little white church from my dream. Recently my uncle, Rock Haynes, who was an incredible photographer, just passed away. My cousins gave me a picture he took of Peggy Cove from his private signed collection. The Lord is operating on your behalf more than your wildest imagination! For me, it was a sweet reminder of my trip to Peggy Cove and that little white church. The Lord was reminding me of what he had promised. My husband would live and not die and declare the works of the Lord. Today my husband has made great strides toward total healing. I know we are almost one hundred percent healed from what the doctor has called an incurable disease. But there's more to come from this beautiful dream.

The Lord always adds endless layers to every encounter you ever experience. I have always translated the word Angelica as meaning an angel or messenger. While preparing for this Bible study, I learned a new meaning based on the plant called Angelica, defined as a tall, aromatic plant of the parsley family, with large leaves and yellowish-green flowers. It is native to North America, used in cooking and herbal medicine. The plant, early 16th century from medieval Latin, was named Angelica because it was believed to be a powerful herb against poisoning and disease. So even now, ten years later, God is still using the blue angel dream to show me amazing, beautiful things he has stored up for me here on earth to discover. I need to start cooking with Angelica!

Discussion Questions

1. Look closer at the throne angels mentioned in the Bible. Discuss what you think they are like and their purpose. You can find details about throne angels here: Ezekiel 1:19 (sphere or wheel angels like Harper in the novel). NOTE:

The wheels ablaze here are angels like Harper mentioned in the book of Ezekiel.

2. When the living beings moved, the wheels beside them moved; when the living beings rose up from the ground, the wheels rose up too. Wherever the spirit would go, they would go, and the wheels would rise up beside them because the spirit of the living being was in the wheel. When the living beings moved, the wheels moved, and when they stopped moving, the wheels stopped. When they rose up from the ground, the wheels rose up from the ground; the wheels rose up beside them because the spirit of the living being was in the wheel.

3. Have you had an encounter with an angel? Describe. Check out these Scriptures to learn more about angels and the hierarchy of angels in the Bible: Rev. 9: 1-2, Rev. 16:5 and Rev. 14:18. These angels have authority over elements like fire, water, and the pit.

4. The angel Michael seems to have an army of angels who report to him in Jude 1:9 and Rev. 12: 7

5. Matthew 18:10 describe angels on assignment for little kids who constantly see the face of the Father (like Harper). In

the Bible, angels are mentioned 114 times, and rankings are mentioned 48 times.

What does this mean for you?

If you believe every word of the Bible like me, it means you believe angels are real. It's important to remember you should never worship angels. Most people who saw angels in the Bible feared them like I did in the dream. They are messengers, so remember—if an angel shows up, they're trying to tell you something. Once at a conference, I had an angel pressing on my forehead for thirty minutes. I didn't know it was an angel, nor did I see an angel, but I described the situation to a friend who I knew had the spiritual gift of discerning spirits. She said, "It's an angel placing a seal on your head." I pressed in through prayer and asked the Holy Spirit for Scripture to verify what she had said, and sure enough, I found Scripture to confirm there is a seal upon the foreheads marked by angels. Scripture confirmed that it is work an angel would do in Rev. 7-18. SOS 8:6 speaks of seals upon your heart, which is the work of the Lord.

My point here is to ask the Holy Spirit for Scripture to confirm all supernatural activity. Don't just take anyone's word for it; dig in and ask for Jesus, the WORD, to confirm all supernatural activity.

Chapter 4

DEMONS

If you study the life of Jesus, you see he was very matter of fact when dealing with demons. He wasn't scared of them. He stood in his authority at every opportunity, and you can too. When I wrote *Over My Dead Body*, one of my goals was to demystify demons. That's why I have Marq, the demon in the novel, focus on operating in legal territory. Even the very word Satan means adversary, which is a job. The job description of an adversary is to accuse a person who committed a crime. What is the offense? Sin. Who paid for the crime? Jesus. In a court of law, you would hire a lawyer to defend you against the authority who is accusing you. Jesus is your lawyer and has already paid all your fines and debt. Remember the wages of sin is death (Romans 6:23).

Many know and understand the Good News (gospel) if they have heard the call of the Holy Spirit when someone explains it to them. What many don't understand is how Jesus walked in great authority. Jesus defeated sin by humbling himself of his divinity (Philippians 2: 5-8), leaving his throne and living a life free of sin by the power of the Holy Spirit. His payment of death covers our sin. We have his power because he gave it to us by saying, "Use my name" (Mk 16:17). I want people to understand an approach to demons that won't freak them out by using their God-given authority in the name of the Lord Jesus Christ.

How do you get a ruling in your favor? You deal with the accuser in legal territory using the same weapons of warfare Jesus used. Jesus was clear. Breaking legal ties is addressed through two avenues—forgiveness (forgive, and you will be forgiven) and repentance (go and sin no more). Once you deal with these two areas, legal rights through sin are void and null. Then by the authority in the name of the Lord Jesus Christ, approach demons like pesky flies you can swat with a flyswatter. Another name for Satan is lord of the flies, but Jesus is the Lord of Lords and the King of Kings. These names for Jesus cover the political and spiritual realms.

I will share one of my personal experiences having to do with demons. If you study the ministry of Jesus, you see every demon he encountered caused sickness. My example has to do with demons of pain. Did you know pain is the name of a group of demons? The definition of pain is suffering, agony, affliction, torture, torment, and depression. Every one of these describes the name for a demon. You get the idea. This is a list of the names of the demons who report to the leader called pain. A strongman if you will.

Demons operate under hierarchies, authorities, and roles (Ephesians 6:12) just as angels do. Ephesians lists the hierarchy in the demonic world as principalities, powers, and rulers of this dark world, and spiritual wickedness in high places. For an example of this in Scripture, take a look at the historical account of the demon Legion (Mark 5:1-20 and Luke 8:26-39).

At the age of twenty-five, I was in a car accident and injured my neck. I spent seven years going to a chiropractor twice a week, dealing with headaches and neck and upper back pain. One day I heard about a local person who had the spiritual gift of healing. Without thinking about my pain, I decided to bring my mother to her for healing prayer for diabetes. After she prayed for my mother, she asked me if I needed prayer for anything. I said, "No, I'm fine," but then I heard the Holy Spirit say, "What about your neck?" I repeated out loud what I heard him say, "What about my neck?" So she laid hands on me and prayed, and the pain I had been carrying around with me for seven years went away immediately. I walked around in astonishment! Living with pain that lifted that fast left me dumbfounded. I was looking from side to side for two weeks trying out my new neck and spine but still unsure if it was real. The Holy Spirit finally said to me, "Kelly, you are well. Believe it and receive it before you lose it." I have not had a problem with my neck and my upper back since.

As you study this topic with the questions to ponder, remember Jesus taught us to deal with demons—not to allow them to have their way.

Remember, they fight harder against someone who knows their authority in Christ. Before you do battle, ask the Holy Spirit to forgive all your sin, cover you by the blood of Jesus, and then use the name of the Lord Jesus Christ to tell them to leave. Ask the Holy Spirit daily to fill you fresh and new with his Spirit to assure the illness or trauma does not return. Mathew 12:45, James 4:7.

Discussion Questions

1. Discuss the hierarchies of demons. Read Ephesians 6:10 and identify the hierarchies of demons in context. I recommend reading a couple of versions of the same text; try the Amplified Version and the New International Version.

In Mathew 8 28-34, Jesus casts out demons:

> When he came to the other side into the country of the Gadarenes, two men who were demon-possessed met him as they were coming out of the tombs. They were so extremely violent no one could pass by that way. And they cried out, saying, "What business do we have with each other, Son of God? Have you come here to torment us before the time?" Now there was a herd of many swine feeding at a distance from them. The demons began to entreat him, saying, "If you are going to cast us out, send us into the herd of swine." And he said to them, "Go!" And they came out and went into the swine, and the whole herd rushed down the steep bank into the sea and perished in the waters. The

herdsmen ran away and went to the city and reported everything, including what had happened to the demoniacs. And behold, the whole city came out to meet Jesus; and when they saw him, they implored him to leave their region.

A few observations by looking up all three accounts of this situation in Matthew, Mark and Luke:

❖ The whole region wanted to hold on to their demonic infestation because the demonic had affected the herd of pigs (they were making money from the Romans who were the only people in the region who ate pork) in Mark 5:1-20. So, they were mad due to financial reasons. Does that sound familiar?

❖ Jesus can banish them to the abyss! Look at Luke 8:26-39. The demons ask Jesus in verse 30 not to banish them or torture them, but we can ask Jesus to banish and torture them when contending against them since it appears they are asking for this not to happen. I would consider this a strategy in prayer.

❖ The spiritual beings knew who Jesus was, but they did not see the future, or they would never have asked to go into the swine. Jesus let them go into the pigs to demonstrate how many were there (2,000 at least). The name Legion is a Roman term representing hierarchy and reporting structures, so you can glean information from that as well.

2. How do you tell when you are dealing with evil? (Hint: violence and bitterness)

3. Do you think demons are visible to humans? Why? Read about this in the Old Testament here: Job 4:15 (can be visible to humans) and the New Testament here: Luke 8:30, Mathew 12:25.

4. Next time you encounter evil through sickness, violence, anger, bitterness, trauma, and all the other names of demonic activity, how will you deal with them based on what Jesus taught us?

Chapter 5

JOHN THE BAPTIST, THE TRINITY AND ANNAS THE HIGH PRIEST

Let's start with the fulfillment of the prophecy about John the Baptist. Mark 1:2-3 (actually three places in the Old Testament but Hebrew tradition was to mention the most well-known source. It was also in Ex. 23:20 and Malachi 3:1). This passage in Mark cites only the prophet Isaiah.

I can't mention John the Baptist without talking about the Trinity. One of the main places in Scripture you get to see the Trinity is in John 1:29, where John testifies Jesus is the Son of God. At the same moment, the dove, representing the Holy Spirit, descends upon Jesus. Then the cherry on the top is the voice of God the Father saying, "This is my son who I am well pleased with." This statement in the ancient Hebrew culture is a term everyone there recognized. When a boy becomes a man in Israel, this is what his father would say, so the community knows he is a representative of his father. The Hebrew people witnessing knew what the term meant. It's the father saying, "If my son shows up and wants to buy something at your shop, he is representing me. If he is conducting business, know that from now on, he is doing business on my behalf. The leaders present knew what the voice of the Father was saying. It meant Jesus had all the power of the Father and is one of the reasons they were so surprised. Remember, some of them heard thunder, but some of them heard the truth. They also knew the Lamb of God meant the sacrifice for sin. Each word spoken by John and the Father had a purpose.

The Trinity

Let me address the baptism of the Holy Spirit one more time. I remind you the Holy Spirit is the Spirit of Jesus. John's testimony was "the one the dove remains on would baptize with the Holy Spirit." I already shared with you in the introduction my supernatural experience of when the Holy Spirit baptized me. If you know Jesus, you know the Father, and if you know the Father and Jesus, you know the Spirit of Jesus. If you know the Holy Spirit, then he will give you gifts of his choosing. We have already discussed the Holy Spirit in 1 Corinthians 12:7 (nine spiritual gifts), Galatians 5:22-23 (nine fruits).

The Trinity in the Old Testament: Genesis 1:1. Elohim is a plural noun. The Hebrew word for God is Elohim. Elohim is a plural noun, but it is used here with a singular verb *bara*. In the remainder of the Old Testament, when Elohim speaks of the true God, it is always used with a singular verb. The conclusion to be drawn is, in some sense, God is both singular and plural. The doctrine of the Trinity states this: within the nature of the one God, there are three eternal persons.

~ Don Stewart, *Blue Letter Bible* [blueletterbible.org]

Genesis 1:26. Let us make man in our image. Genesis 3:22.

Isaiah 48:16-17 (Verse 16. God the Son is speaking and identifies the Father and the Spirit). Isaiah 63:16, Malachi 2:10 (the Father), Isaiah 9:6 (the Son). We have already studied the Holy Spirit in 1 Corinthians 12:7 (nine Spiritual Gifts), Galatians 5:22-23 (nine fruits).

Annas, the High Priest, was the first person the temple guards brought Jesus to for the beginning of six illegal trials. He was the primary person who pushed to have Jesus arrested and murdered. He is one of the central people in the novel. All the lies of the enemy hinged on his decisions. I have Scriptures below for you to get to know what the Bible says about Annas as you are reading about him in the novel. I used Annas because I wanted to demonstrate all the prophecies Jesus fulfilled and what lies Annas had to tell himself not to believe Jesus was the Messiah. I also want to point out Annas either knew Jesus fulfilled prophecies or had to have learned over time. It's hard to believe the sun would reach a standstill and the veil in the temple would be torn, yet Annas did not question the supernatural phenomenon.

Caiaphas prophesied about him and Annas had to know the prophecy.

Read John 18:12-14.

Then the Roman soldiers under their commander, joined by the Jewish police, seized Jesus and tied him up. They took him first to Annas, father-in-law of Caiaphas. Caiaphas was the Chief Priest that year. It was Caiaphas who had advised the Jews it was to their advantage that one-person die for the people. Simon Peter and another disciple followed Jesus. The Chief Priest knew that other disciple, and so he went in with Jesus to the Chief Priest's courtyard. Peter had to stay outside. Then the other disciple went out, spoke to the doorkeeper, and got Peter in. The young woman who was the doorkeeper said to Peter, "Aren't you one of this man's disciples? "He said, "No, I'm not." The servants and police had made a fire because of the cold and were huddled there warming themselves. Peter stood with them, trying to get warm

The Interrogation

John 18:19-24.

Annas interrogated Jesus regarding his disciples and his teaching. Jesus answered, "I've spoken openly in public. I've taught regularly in meeting places and the Temple, where the Jews all come together. Everything has been out in the open. I've said nothing in secret. So why are you treating me like a conspirator? Question those who have been listening to me. They know well what I have said. My teachings have all been aboveboard." When he said this, one of the policemen standing there slapped Jesus across the face, saying, "How dare you speak to the Chief Priest like that!" Jesus replied, "If I've said something wrong, prove it. But if I've spoken the plain truth, why this slapping around?" Then Annas sent him, still tied up, to the Chief Priest Caiaphas.

In the back pages of a small green Bible I was using, it had a list of many of the prophecies fulfilled by Jesus, with Scripture references from the Old Testament and the New Testament. When I saw the list, I wanted others to realize Annas had to know the truth; after all, it was his job to know prophecy and watch for Messiah. I vowed to use the list while writing the novel to show Jesus fulfilled prophecy.

Discussion Questions

1. Mark 1:2-3 gives us an example of prophecy fulfilled about John the Baptist.

    Then John the Baptist testifies about Jesus, the Father and the Holy Spirit—the Trinity—in John 1:29.

    The next day, John saw Jesus coming toward him and said, "Look, the Lamb of God, who takes away the sin of the world! This is the one I meant when I said, 'A man who comes after me has surpassed me because he was before me.' I myself did not know him, but the reason I came baptizing with water was that he might be revealed to Israel." Then John gave this testimony: "I saw the Spirit come down from heaven as a dove and remain on him. And I myself did not know him, but the one who sent me to baptize with water told me, 'The man on whom you see the Spirit come down and remain is the one who will baptize with the Holy Spirit.' I have seen, and I testify that this is God's Chosen One."

    We also see the Trinity in the following places:

    ❖ The Old Testament in Genesis 1.

    ❖ The quote from *Blue Letter Bible* (page 26 of this study)

- ❖ Genesis 1:26. Let us make man in our image.

- ❖ Genesis 3:22

- ❖ Isaiah 48:16-17 (In verse 16, God the Son is speaking and identifies the Father and the Spirit).

- ❖ Isaiah 63:16

- ❖ Malachi 2:10 (the Father)

- ❖ Isaiah 9:6 (the Son)

2. The Trinity is often brought to question. What are some of the questions about the Trinity that made you dig into Scripture to find the truth?

3. Can you think of compelling reasons why Annas would have allowed this trial against the rules during Passover? (See Scripture about Annas: John 18:12-24. The first of six illegal trials. Prophecy fulfilled.)

4. What questions do you have about Annas? Do you think he will be in heaven?

5. If Jesus only did what he saw the Father doing, and Jesus asked the Father to forgive them for they know not what they do, do you think Annas is forgiven?

6. Do you feel forgiven? Read Luke 6:37. Forgive, and you will be forgiven. Psalm 103:10-12 talks about the benefits of forgiveness.

What does this mean for you?

This chapter is about solidifying your faith in what prophecy has said about Jesus. If you can grasp the truth from the Old Testament prophesized word and match it to the New Testament, it helps you explain the facts to those who have questions as to why you have your faith. Knowing what the word says about Jesus in the Old Testament, thousands of years before Jesus walked the earth, should build your confidence by leaps and bounds.

Chapter 6

SYMBOLS AND TYPES AND HUSBANDS AND WIVES

Jesus not only spoke in symbolic language in the New Testament by using parables, but when he talked to the disciples to explain his life, death, and resurrection, he used symbols. The very names he used to describe himself were symbolic. There are twenty-four references in the book of John where Jesus calls himself the I AM. Notice it's the same name God told Moses to call him when talking to the burning bush. God also used I AM to explain to Pharaoh who he was in Exodus 3:14. When Jesus called himself this, it set off the religious leaders because they thought it was blasphemy. However, Jesus demonstrated with signs and wonders he was who he said he was.

A symbol is an object that stands for something else. I studied symbols and their various kinds in my college classes, but most of my study in symbolic language has been focused on dreams in the Bible. For the last ten years, I've gained an understanding of dreams with the help of the Holy Spirit, who is the interpreter of all dreams. I've also trained myself to think in symbolic language. I study dreams in the Bible because God speaks in symbolic language throughout the Old Testament. Not only in dreams but also in poetry, dark sayings (hidden meanings), and Psalms.

One kind of symbol in the Bible is called a *type* (or *shadow)*, which is a situation occurring in the Old Testament that points to (foreshadows) what is to come with Jesus. For example, Jonah spent three days in the belly of the whale. This is a "type" or a "shadow" of Jesus spending three days in the tomb defeating death. Jonah overcame, as did Jesus. Daniel in the lions' den is a *type* or *shadow* of Jesus shutting the mouth of the enemy while being tested in the desert. David defeating Goliath is another example of a *type* symbol, in which a real historical event paralleled what Jesus would do once he left his throne to come to earth. Jesus symbolically defeated death, a *type* of giant that taunts God's people. When you start digging deep into your Bible, you'll find a golden thread of Scripture that identifies these types or foreshadowings. Romans 1:20, which says, "All of Creation speaks of God's glory," means once you understand how God speaks in symbolic language, you should be able to see God in every circumstance. You can find him symbolically in a leaf or a seed. Get creative as you study the word of God by asking the Holy Spirit to show you the golden thread.

Husbands and Wives

One of my goals with this book was to show a young married couple working together toward a God-sized assignment. I wanted Joel and Hannah to display a married couple who were a true team. I hoped Joel's character toward Hannah would shine through and symbolically illustrate a *type* or foreshadowing of Jesus. Jesus is for his bride, the church, as described below by Paul and outlined by Moses. Ephesians 5:25: "For husbands, this means love your wives, just as Christ loved the church. He gave up his life for her."

In Ephesians 5:33, Paul writes, "Let each one of you in particular so love his own wife as himself, and let the wife see she respects her husband."

If all husbands loved as Jesus does and all wives (churches) respected their husbands (Jesus), there would be no divorce and no church or people division. We should be praying daily for unity in the church, including agreement on bringing in those in Israel who still don't realize Yeshua is who he said he is.

Discussion Questions

Literary devices found in the Bible include **symbols** and **types**: A *symbol* is an object that stands for something else. A *type* (also called a *shadow*) is a situation occurring in the Old Testament that foreshadows or points to what's to come with Jesus.

In Exodus 3:14, God—the God of Abraham, Isaac, and Jacob—told Moses to tell them his name is "I AM." See what Jesus said in John 8:56-58. This is one of the first significant times the religious leaders were incited to destroy Jesus.

In the book of John, Jesus used symbolic words to describe himself starting with "I AM" fifty-four times: *I AM the bread of life. I AM the Son of Man. I AM the true vine.*

Here are twenty-four references to him using them clearly: John 4:26; 6:20; 6:35; 6:41; 6:48; 6:51; 7:28; 7:29; 7:33; 7:34; 7:36; 8:12; 8:16; 8:18; 8:23 (twice); 8:24; 8:28; 8:58; 9:5; 10:7; 10:9; 10:11; 10:14; 10:36; 11:25; 12:26; 13:13; 13:19; 13:33; 14:3; 14:6; 14:9; 15:1; 15:5; 16:32; 17:11; 17:14; 17:16; 17:24; 18:5; 18:6; 18:8; 18:37; 19:21.

1. What is your favorite name for God? The Almighty (Gen.17:1,2), Everlasting God (Psalm 48:14), or one of the names Jesus used in the above listed Scriptures?

2. Read Romans 1:20. All of creation speaks of God's glory. What have you seen in nature that has spoken to you about God?

3. Name a situation that spoke symbolically to you about God's nature.

4. Husbands and wives: Jesus is for his bride, the church, as described below by Paul and outlined by Moses. Ephesians 5:25: "For husbands, this means love your wives, just as Christ loved the church. He gave up his life for her."

   In Ephesians 5:33, Paul writes, "Let each one of you in particular so love his own wife as himself, and let the wife see that she respects her husband."

   If all husbands loved as Jesus does and all wives respected their husbands, do you think there would be divorce? Why?

What does this mean for you?

You absolutely *can* hear from the Holy Spirit on any dream. Ask the Holy Spirit to reveal what your dreams mean or even unusual circumstances you notice in your waking life. The same way he speaks symbolically in the Bible and in dreams, he also speaks in our daily lives. Ask God to speak to you symbolically. Play games with the Holy Spirit by asking him for object lessons. For example, when I asked the Holy Spirit to remind me daily to spend time confessing my sin to him, he highlighted to me the squidgy in the shower that I use to remove the shower scum that accumulates daily, and he used it as an example to remind me a daily confession will keep sin from growing in my life. He used a squidgy to remind me he is the God who forgives my sin!

Chapter 7

Josephus, Gentile Saviours and Theophanies

I like to think of Josephus as a Jewish reporter or an eyewitness from that era. He was born in 37 AD and died in 100 AD. He wrote books that recorded war history for Israel but also was involved in the fall of Jerusalem. He is a vital eyewitness of what happened when Titus marched on Jerusalem in 70 AD. He was also crucial to future Christians because he wrote the only account outside of the Gospels about Jesus and his crucifixion. Although he wasn't born until after the resurrection, he would have had the chance to speak to first-hand eyewitnesses in Jerusalem as a young reporter. It also appears Josephus believed Jesus was Messiah.

> About this time, there lived Jesus, a wise man if indeed one
> ought to call him a man. For he was one who performed
> surprising deeds and was a teacher of such people as accept
> the truth gladly. He won over many Jews and many of the
> Greeks. He was the Messiah. And when, upon the

accusation of the principal men among us, Pilate had condemned him to a cross, those who had first come to love him did not cease. He appeared to them spending a third day restored to life, for the prophets of God had foretold these things and a thousand other marvels about him. And the tribe of the Christians, so-called after him, has still to this day not disappeared.

～ Jewish Antiquities, 18.3.3 §63 (based on the translation of Louis H. Feldman, *The Loeb Classical Library*)

It's astounding! Josephus is amazed here in this passage that the tribe of Yeshua's followers had not disappeared. He knew this was a rare occurrence. Josephus recorded this around 93 AD. Reading between the lines, Josephus is saying; "Look, sixty years later and people still believe in Yeshua!" If it was a miracle at sixty years, imagine what Josephus would say today, 2,000 years later!

While in prison after being taken as a prisoner from the suicide compact fiasco (mentioned in the novel), Josephus convinced Vespasian (one of the Cesars) that he had the gift of prophecy.

One of my first experiences hearing from God—the definition of prophecy—is what helped me realize how real he is. I asked the Holy Spirit to tell me who in the Bible I remind him of. He said to me *Naomi*.

My first reaction was "NAOMI? She's old!" I was quite young back then.

Then the Lord said to me, *But she helped my daughters find their Kinsman Redeemer* (see book of Ruth; Boaz is a shadow of Jesus).

I replied, "I'll take it!" I was fine with that job. I also asked him what my new name would be, and I heard the name Deidre so clear. The meaning of the name in Gaelic is *daughter*. I know I did not come up with this name in my mind. I am a daughter to the King. A princess of heaven.

Practice this in your quiet time with the Holy Spirit. Ask him for a picture, a word, scene, or even to whisper something to you in a still small voice. Get a journal to write down what he tells you.

The Holocaust and Gentile Saviors

For my book I researched Gentile saviors or what are known as Righteous Among the Nations. These are non-Jews who risked their lives to save Jews during the Holocaust. I began researching at the Holocaust Museum in Jerusalem and found there were more than 26,000 names to pull from for this section of my novel. I could only bring to light any details on a couple who were a team at the Catholic Church in Assisi, and one Irena Sendler (Jolanta).

The team in Assisi helped hide the Jewish people by creating Italian legal papers to smuggle them out of Italy. Italy was part of the Axis of Evil, so the Jewish people were trying to get out since the beginning of World War II. The beautiful mountain town of Assisi did not have any Jewish residents before the war, so it was an ideal place to hide those trying to escape.

To represent Irena, I used Ben, the bus driver. I wanted to include her for her amazing accomplishments. There is a beautiful play put together about Irena by some high school kids from Union Town, Kansas, called *Life in a Jar*. These high school kids performed it around the country and were also allowed to visit Irena in Poland in the year 2000, before she died in 2008. She and a team of twenty people rescued 2,500 children from the Warsaw ghetto. She was up for a Nobel Peace Prize and lost it to Al Gore.

Theophanies

I wanted more than one theophany in the book. A theophany is a tangible manifestation of God to the human senses. In its most restrictive sense, it is a visible appearance of God, as in the Old Testament period, often but not always in human form. Some theophanies can be found in your Discussion Questions at the end of the chapters, and also at the end of this section.

Frequently, the term "glory of the Lord" reflects a theophany, as in Exodus 24:16-18; the "pillar of cloud" has a similar function in Exodus 33:9. In the Bible, a signal that a theophany is coming are the words "the Lord came down," as in Genesis 11:5, Exodus 34:5, Numbers 11:25 and 12:5.

Some Bible commentators believe whenever someone received a visit from "the angel of the Lord," this was, in fact, the pre-incarnate Christ. These appearances are in Genesis 16:7-14, Genesis 22:11-18, Judges 5:23, 2 Kings 19:35, and other passages. Other commentators believe these were, in fact, angelophanies, or appearances of angels. While there are no indisputable Christophanies in the Old Testament, every theophany wherein God takes on human form foreshadows the incarnation, where God took the form of a man to live among us as Emmanuel, "God with us" (Matthew 1:23).

Discussion Questions

1. Does Josephus as a witness help you believe the four Gospel accounts even further? Learning this grew my faith by leaps and bounds. What questions does it raise for you?

2. Josephus used the gift of prophecy to get out of prison. What did Paul say about prophesy? Read 1 Cor 14:3: But he who prophesies speaks to men for their edification, encouragement, and comfort. Read 1 Cor 14:31: For you can all prophesy in turn so that everyone may be instructed and encouraged.

3. Get quiet with the Holy Spirit and ask him to tell you something. Ask God who in the Bible you remind him of. Once you get a name, look up the qualities of that person in the Bible and talk to him about it. Ask him for more insight as to how you are like that person. Did you hear something? If not, keep asking.

4. What would you do if you were living back then and you knew they were killing Jewish people?

Theophanies:

The Lord appeared to Abraham on his arrival in the land God had promised to him and his descendants (Genesis 12:7-9).

One day, Abraham had some visitors: two angels and God himself. He invited them to come to his home, and he and Sarah entertained them (Genesis 18:1-33).

Many commentators believe this could also be a Christophany, a pre-incarnate appearance of Christ.

Jacob wrestled with what appeared to be a man, but was God (Genesis 32:28-30). This was probably a Christophany.

God appeared to Moses in the form of a burning bush, telling him precisely what he wanted him to do (Exodus 3:2 - 4:17).

God appeared to Moses with Aaron and his sons and the seventy elders (Exodus 24:9-11).

God appeared to Moses and Joshua in the transfer of leadership to Joshua (Deuteronomy 31:14-15).

God answered Job out of the storm and spoke at great length in answer to Job's questions (Job 38–42).

What does this mean for you?

The topics we discussed today and throughout the study is to help grow your faith. Josephus was a fifth witness along with Matthew, Mark, Luke, and John, of what happened to Jesus. The four Gospels were written anywhere from 65-95 AD. The fact that Josephus had the gift of prophecy should make you want it for yourselves as well. Ask the Holy Spirit for the gift of prophecy since Paul said we all can prophesy. As far as the theophanies are concerned, I hope they'll help you enjoy the incredible treasure the Israelites preserved for us with the Old Testament. I hope you'll read it with new eyes and a new appreciation, so much so that Romans 11:11 will be part of your daily prayer for the Jewish people. Ask the Lord to give you the wisdom of how you might help the Jewish people come to know Yeshua as their Messiah.

Chapter 8

CONCLUSION AND FUN TIDBITS

You should have completed reading the novel by now. To kick off a book club like discussion, I want to share with you some fun tidbits of my research and how I used it to complete the adventure in the novel:

Hitler's UFO

MI6, the secret British intelligence agency, reported in 1948 after the war that Hitler had used a special unidentified flying machine over Mount Ararat to take pictures in an attempt to find Noah's Ark. This topic fascinated me. I used this piece of history to show Hitler was working with Nephilim. I did not indicate in the novel if Hitler realized he was working with Nephilim or not, but the running thread of a stolen angel ark that looked like a huge cylinder large enough to black out the sky in Jerusalem formed a springboard from this research.

The quote used by Aubrey MacKenzie

In the news report at the end of the book is an authentic quote: "The discovery of Noah's Ark would be the greatest archaeological find in human history, the greatest event since the resurrection of Christ, and it would alter all the currents of scientific thought." It is attributed to G. Grosvenor, *National Geographic* editor. The idea of an editor from *National Geographic* giving this kind of weight to finding Noah's Ark pushed me toward wanting Joel to find Noah's Ark so I could use this great quote. For the record, I agree with G. Grosvenor.

The flood and Nephilim

The courtroom conclusion based around the Scripture 1 Peter 3:18-20:

For Christ also suffered once for sins, the righteous for the unrighteous, to bring you to God. He was put to death in the body but made alive in the Spirit. After being made alive, he went and proclaimed to the imprisoned spirits—to those who were disobedient long ago when God waited patiently in the days of Noah while the ark was built. In it, only a few people, eight in all, were saved through water,

In this passage, Peter is saying Jesus is ministering to those who had died before Noah's Ark when the land was full of giants (Nephilim). This topic sparked great interest for me, and I was excited to find a way to include Marq as one of those half-breed Nephilim spirits who might have a chance at redemption. Even the Catholic Church says in the Apostles' Creed that Jesus went to hell to minister to souls. It does not say if they were half-bred or not, and it was of great interest for me to know the land was so full of Nephilim that Noah and his family were the only people not impacted by the polluted gene pool.

Real-life rescuers of Assisi

In Assisi, there was a real group of priests and nuns who helped rescue 300 Jewish people. While on vacation in Assisi, I toured the dome-shaped room and print shop where the false identification papers were processed to help people escape the Nazis.

Dreams

I have spent many years trying to understand symbolic meanings in dreams. Rachel's dream about Spence was a foreshadow of Rachel becoming a believer in Yeshua (Jesus in Hebrew) as the Messiah. The dream was about swimming in blood and his robe turning white, which is mentioned in Isaiah 61:1 in Scripture, describing people being washed by the blood of Jesus and given white robes symbolizing garments of salvation.

Harper the angel's background

I have always been fascinated with angel food and manna. I love the fact that manna means "what is it?" When I wrote about the angel Harper, I was at my mother-in-law's house in Davidson, North Carolina. I had been there a few days writing when I got the angel/manna/waffles concept and idea. At one point that weekend, I needed to take a break so I went for a walk and I realized the name of the street she lived on was Harper Lee, who is the author of *To Kill A Mockingbird*. It made me realize the name Harper was a great name for an angel, which is where I got the idea to use the throne angel and talk about how Harper's voice sounded like a harp (but he didn't play the harp). So, Harper is named after Harper Lee, not the musical instrument.

Nephilim

I did a ton of research on the Nephilim. My dad was one of the reasons I dug into this topic so much. He asked me about Nephilim on several occasions, and I decided to dig in so I could try to help him understand Genesis chapter six. There are two different approaches by biblical scholars on the topic. After in-depth research, I chose one of the theories for the demon. I decided Marq would be a disembodied spirit of a Nephilim. I covered this topic in-depth earlier in the demon chapter in this book but wanted to mention why I decided to bring in the subject. I still want to know how they got their different personalities, which are based on assignments. I will press in on this topic for the sequel. Is it possible when they fell to earth from the third heaven they were assigned the opposite of what their assignment in heaven was before the fall? I never would've thought of the concept of a demon having a personality or an attribute if the Lord hadn't shown me how to be delivered from the demon of trauma after my husband's emergency heart situation.

Important dates

According to theologians, Jesus was born around the year 4 A.D. (C.E.). Titus marched on the temple in Jerusalem forty years to the exact week of the crucifixion of Jesus. Anniversaries will prove to be important in my future books.

Turin

I was excited to learn about Turin in my research. While writing the chapter on the Menace of Venice, I learned Napoleon did try to get the Jewish people in Italy to "become French." He wanted the bankers to give up being bankers. The wealthy farmers in charge of money indeed became the money lenders. They were great farmers and decision-makers. They naturally made tons of money, so they offered loans. Historically, Jewish people become bankers because they seem to have a knack at generating provision. The Lord told them in the Scriptures they would be the lender, not the debtor. I don't understand why people are surprised the Jewish people were the bankers. God's word said it, and I believe it. It goes to show you most of the time when Jewish people are persecuted, it boils down to jealousy. People were and still seem to be jealous because the Jews were blessed. But remember, Romans 11:11 says that Paul believes the Gentiles will provoke the Jewish people to jealousy because of the blessing Gentiles will receive from the Lord Jesus Christ as Messiah through signs and wonders. I want the Jewish people back in the fold, and it will come to pass based on Ephesians 2:14-16 (see what the apostle Paul said about "one new man"):

> For He Himself is our peace, who has made both one, and has broken down the middle wall of separation, having abolished in His flesh the enmity, that is, the law of commandments contained in ordinances, so as to create in Himself one new man from the two, thus making peace, 16 and that He might reconcile them both to God in one body through the cross, thereby putting to death the enmity.

Story-Related Questions for Final Book Club Meeting

1. What part of the story did you relate to the most?
2. If this was not a novel and you discovered the box yourself, what would you do with the box?

3. Which character did you relate to the most? Joel, Hannah, Naomi, Rabbi Jacob, Harper or Marq?

4. Have you considered the difference between fallen angels and demons? What do you think the difference is, if any?

5. Have you ever had an encounter with an angel or a demon? Discuss.

6. A root of bitterness causes grudges, anger, and an inability to forgive. Consider and discuss times when you may have found yourself with a root of bitterness like Joel's father Ely. Learn more at Hebrews 12:15 and Deuteronomy 29:18.

7. What did you think of Joel and Hannah's relationship? What stood out to you?

8. The theme surrounding the Key of David is one of authority. Do you understand authority? For example, when a police officer pulls you over, he or she has the power to do so, and you comply because you understand authority. How does the earthly concept of authority translate to your Kingdom authority as a son or daughter of Yeshua? You can dig deeper at Isaiah 22:22, Luke 9:12 and Luke 1:3.

9. What do you think Rabbi Jacobs's conclusion was about the Messiah after finding what he had been looking for his whole life?

10. Have you ever considered what it would be like to be in the courtroom of heaven? If not, take some time to imagine and discuss what you might experience.

11. Read John 14:2; it talks of the many rooms in heaven. Name a place you hope to find in heaven.

I HOPE YOU HAVE ENJOYED THIS STUDY!

I pray your time spent studying the word of God and the concepts in the novel has been encouraging and you have gained some new insights to deepen your relationship with the Lord Jesus Christ. If you have questions for me, please do not hesitate to send me an email at kellyfitzgeraldfowler@gmail.com or find me on social media on FB, Twitter, Instagram or Pinterest @kellyffowler

A Note from Kelly to Bible Study Leaders

Thank you for the sacrifice you are making to help guide others through a Bible study. I am praying for you as you walk into a leadership role. If you have been a leader for a while, you understand the need for prayer coverage. If this is your first time, please find others to cover you in prayer. You need support whenever you step out for the Kingdom of God.

Ask the Holy Spirit to come in significant measure to your gathering. The Holy Spirit led me to start each week with ten minutes of soaking music, which he directed me to choose. Ask the Holy Spirit with what music he would like you to begin the first ten minutes of your study. Soaking music helps prepare hearts and fosters an atmosphere to hear from him. If he tells you to play worship music, then follow his lead. Soaking is a quiet resting time with the Lord and a specific type of music that allows you to experience a peaceful measure of the presence of the Holy Spirit. I highly recommend you do this as well. If choosing music is hard for you, ask the Holy Spirit to send you someone gifted in choosing music to help.

This study covers many levels of concepts that vary from simple to complex. Be okay with not knowing the answer to every question. I ask the Holy Spirit to give you the wisdom and knowledge you need to answer questions that come up. Be humble enough to say, "I don't know, but I will see what I can find out about that topic." It's perfectly fine not to be able to answer every question on the spot. Please email me if you run into a problem in this area at kellyfitzgeraldfowler@gmail.com

Greet each person every week. The Lord has handpicked those he has put in your circle of influence. Pray for them regularly and get to know them.

Let them know on your first meeting there will be obstacles in their way to make it to your class. Whenever anyone wants to dig deeper into their understanding of Scripture, the enemy will find ways to keep them from coming back to the study. Encourage them to be prepared and to recognize why there will be challenges and how to overcome them by putting their foot down and being committed to come to the class no matter what. Pray against the schemes of the enemy in their lives.

Be sure to have plenty of rest and time to refuel. Spend time with God. You will need to be full if you are going to pour into others' lives.

Build time in the class for them to talk also. People need to process what they are learning. When you ask them questions, try to get them to speak to one another. Make sure you are not dominating the conversation.

Each week I will give you topics, questions, and Scriptures to use to dig deeper with those in your class. If you're leading the class, I recommend you use some of the Scripture for class discussion. In most cases, I'll try to give you a Scripture from the Old Testament (OT) and the New Testament (NT), so you can share and learn how prophecy was fulfilled from hundreds and even thousands of years before Jesus walked the earth. Encourage your students to do some home study if they have time.

I pray you enjoy the topics and discussions I have chosen to cover. Blessings!

Kelly

www.ingramcontent.com/pod-product-compliance
Lightning Source LLC
Chambersburg PA
CBHW071930020426
42331CB00010B/2795